Mapping the Road Less Traveled

A Guide to Running for Public Office

By: G.W. Pomichter

G.W. Pomichter

Contents

G.W. Pomichter

Introduction

A political campaign is a complex, if short-lived, business, and it can never be completely formulated. It is most like trying to estimate the combination of a lock. Each candidate requires a specific one-of-a-kind combination to succeed. The tools and strategies contained herein are not meant to replace qualified campaign staff members, managers or good common sense, but to enhance these and provide administrative guidelines to reduce costly mistakes.

Politics is a difficult and demanding profession and requires, like any other endeavor, a high degree of personal commitment and an aptitude for the intricacies of public policy. This aptitude is not a guarantee for success in campaigning, though.

Campaigns who utilize the tools contained within these pages should also consider the expert help of a professional campaign manager. While many candidates prefer the "hands-on" help of family and friends, one of the foremost tenants of good campaigning is to realize that candidates are more often public policy "buffs" and just as they would ask citizens to allow them to use their talents to serve in public office, they can be best served by those who have more sharpened and highly tuned campaigning skills. As you will read, there are plenty of duties and responsibilities for close supporters. One of the many roles of professional support is to act as a kind of "devil's advocate," and provide an objective point of view that those who are dedicated supporters might not see, or could be hesitant to point out.

Why Run for Office?

Before beginning, it is important that both the candidate and campaign team have a clear understanding of the process in which they are entering and have a sincere desire, with this understanding, to proceed.

Campaigning for public office requires focus and determination, and it can stress both financial and emotional resources. After suffering these trials, winning candidates earn the privilege of holding a demanding and very public profession in politics.

One political analyst humorously described this profession, saying, "It is a profession in which the name is very telling." He

9

went on to explain, "The word can be taken in two parts: Poly, meaning many; and tics, meaning blood sucking animals."

So why do people choose to endure these rigors?

Political science experts define politics as "the struggle or competition for power." But the reason many seek public office is in the finer points of that broader definition. To understand what motivates these unique individuals, we must begin by understanding what political power is, and how it can be used.

Political power can be best defined as the ability to influence or control the behaviors of others. This power can be achieved only by first obtaining the consent of those over whom power is wielded. The United States' historical "Declaration of Independence" notes that governments "derive their just power through the consent of the governed." History reminds one that consent and power can be gained through a variety of methods, including force of arms, inherited authority and, in a democratic republic such as that in the United States, through an electoral process.

Understanding what power consists of and how it is attained is only the beginning, though. More often than not, candidates are motivated by the specific uses of this power within a given social structure. For example, a candidate may perceive the political structure itself as problematic and wish to use the power that accompanies campaign victory to alter that structure — to change the system itself.

Candidates for municipal or county offices may want to improve the level of local police or fire service, while candidates for state legislative offices may be more interested in affecting broader social policies such as making changes to state laws or improving schools. Some federal candidates may want to work to improve national defense or implement more global social policies such as meeting national medical needs. During campaigning, at one time or another, almost all say they will reduce waste and make government more efficient.

The U.S. political structure has been designed to accommodate all of these uses of political power. Its stated faith in the principal of self-governance, as well as in the citizen lawmaker, opens the door for a diverse group of people to participate in the process, bringing with them a wide variety of expertise in many subject areas. Throughout American history, this diversity has often put the right expertise in a position to respond to some of the world's most challenging problem.

Despite the many reasons candidates choose to seek office and to compete for power, one thing that most candidates have in common is that they prefer studying government policy over political campaigning. For this reason, the jobs of candidate and elected official differ greatly and the tools used by the former must be sound in order to achieve the later. Regardless of what motivates a candidate, there are some universal tools that campaigns can use to ensure that any citizen, with sufficient interest in affecting public policy, can wield the power needed to affect change within a given social group by becoming an elected official.

General Knowledge:

Candidates entering public service should always have a general knowledge of public service and of the community they wish to serve. This knowledge can be most easily categorized in three areas: District/Local knowledge, Office/Service Knowledge and Current Events Knowledge.

District/Local

A candidate who wishes to serve in elected office should have a working knowledge of the district or geographic area they wish to serve. This knowledge consists of more than the numeric data that the campaign will use to target voters. It should most effectively consist of a knowledge of local landmarks, large commercial or business interests and industries, and a familiarity with geo-political and social attitudes. For instance, a candidate whose geographic area includes multiple airports or an aircraft manufacturing company, whose constituents may be largely employed by these entities, may benefit from knowledge of aviation terms or industry concerns. Likewise, a candidate whose constituency includes large numbers of union members or rural farmers, should have a working knowledge of the top concerns of these very divergent social groups.

Office/Service

A candidate wishing to serve in any elected office that sets or contributes to public policy should be well versed in the office and level of participation in which they will, if successful, be party to.

If, for example, a legislator is to be responsible for voting on or producing local, state or even federal budget issues, it is wise for a candidate to become as familiar as possible with the most recent budget for the particular government entity. Similarly, a candidate who might be asked to vote upon local zoning changes or business licensing, might study past and recent decisions about these issues made by the government upon which the candidate is asking to serve. This familiarity will help the candidate to avoid dramatic promises they might not be able to keep from the office they seek. It will further set a candidate apart from a less informed or knowledgeable opponent.

Current Events:

While candidates are most often and reasonably interested in events and activities that are subject to the office they seek, it is a mistake not to have a basic grasp of current events at other levels of influence. In fact, national or state trends often play a vital role in shaping a particular population's perspective of local events. For this reason, candidates should familiarize themselves daily with the happenings that are most talked about or might affect these perceptions. As is expected of any person seeking public office, candidates should develop opinions about these issues, but should be wary of posting, publishing or otherwise promoting these opinions publicly, as a candidate's position on issues that are not affected by the office being sought, can impact one's election to that office. Instead, carefully thought out opinions about current events, which are consistent with the campaign's message should be prepared, and only referred to when solicited.

Understanding Campaign Laws

While America's most visible political campaigns are often governed by federal laws and guidelines, such as those that limit contributions to congressional candidates, or define Political Action Committees and regulate Presidential candidates, most of the laws that govern elections are made at the state level.

The U.S. Constitution very specifically delegates the role of officiating elections to each state, and as such, laws that pertain to most elections are made and enforced in the state where an election is held.

15

These state laws can govern everything from the amount of money a campaign may receive, or that an individual, company or political entity may contribute, to the exact language that must be present in political advertising disclaimers.

The chief source of information with regard to political election laws is often the state's Department of State, Division of Elections, Board of Elections or other state election officials. Since each state is different, all candidates and campaign staffers are encouraged to research the laws specific to a candidate's state.

Federal laws responsible for further governing the election of members of both houses of congress and the executive branch are best accessed through the Federal Election Commission or FEC as it is commonly referred.

Campaigns for higher state or federal office should consider retaining legal counsel with election law experience when circumstances allow.

A Good Beginning

A "campaign" is defined as a series of military operations taking place in one area over a particular period, intended to achieve a specific objective. Of course, in politics, the roots of this word have been largely forgotten amidst the trappings of civility. However, a campaign is none-the-less a tactical and militant operation that must be conducted with precision and discipline if it is to succeed. To be successful, a political campaign must include three crucial elements. As in a military campaign, a political campaign must begin with good planning, which includes proper message development, financial planning and budgeting as well as identifying targeted portions of the electorate for obtainable victories. The

17

operation must then look to the specific weapons that will be used to secure these victories, such as advertising media and volunteers. The final phase of the campaign is the assault. During the assault a campaign's message will be delivered using a variety of identified media and a small army of supporters who are committed to ensuring the campaign's success.

Before the campaign can begin in earnest, candidates and campaign workers must plan for a long and sometimes arduous battle. Planning for a political campaign can be broken into three categories. It is first essential to develop the overall message of the campaign. This will include identifying a candidate's strengths and weaknesses as well as those of any opponents. Once a campaign message is developed the winning campaign focuses on identifying specific portions of the electorate that can be convinced to support the candidate. These strategic planning steps are the heart of a good campaign. Without proper planning, the campaign will flounder in a sea of reactionary tactics and eventually fail. Since the goal of any successful political campaign is to achieve consent from a majority of the electorate, it is then necessary to decide what financial costs will be incurred and are acceptable by the campaign, as well as

identifying possible sources for the money needed.

G.W. Pomichter

Developing a Campaign Message

The campaign's message should be a single statement or paragraph that uses the most positive language available to describe a candidate's beliefs, personality and qualifications for the office sought.

Developing a successful campaign message can be the one of the most difficult challenges faced by the campaign staff and the candidate. While there are many ways to develop this message, since it will be used to distinguish the candidate from opponents, identify the candidate to supporters and will spread widely throughout the community, your campaign message is one of the most important tools.

When developing the campaign message, there are four considerations that should be the center of team discussions.

1. What do we want to say about our candidate: What are the most positive attributes of the candidate?

2. What will our opponents say about our candidate: What are the most negative attributes of the candidate?

3. What will our opponents say about their candidate: What are your opponent's most positive attributes?

4. What will we say about our opponent's candidate: What are your opponent's most relevant negatives?

After identifying these vital points, begin to consider individual words that will point out the candidate's positives, while relatively negating the candidate's negatives. In some cases, the campaign's message can also serve to distinguish between the candidate and the opposition by highlighting elements of a candidate that may be contrary to the opponent's negatives.

It is important to remember that the campaign message is not a slogan. It is more appropriately compared to a thesis about the candidate that will be repeatedly supported by all other claims and statements made by the campaign. A slogan may be used in some campaigns, and should be supported by the campaign message. It is critical for the campaign to remain focused, and to use advertising and marketing media to reinforce a consistent campaign message.

G.W. Pomichter

The Electorate:

Voters that your campaign will be targeting will fall into many specific and unique categories. For different elections, there are different target audiences. As you examine the illustration below, realize that while a candidate's message will be consistent, and their ideas will not very often change, the voting audience a campaign will speak to will change from the primary to the general election. For this reason, the campaign should include portions of the candidate's platform that are audience specific.

In primary elections, it is important that candidates put emphasis on aspects of the campaign message that appeal to a narrow field of voters. In these elections candidates must appeal to their partisan loyal voters. While this concern should not dictate a candidate's point of view, it should help to narrow the over all campaign message to the components that will have greatest interest from these constituencies.

For Example: a Republican candidate may believe in maintaining the lowest possible taxes, while spending on social programs in a very open and accountable way.

These candidates will most often in a primary focus the campaign message on lower taxes, but in the general election may choose to focus on a plan for more accountable spending. The overall message is consistent, but the focus of the message speaks to the varying parts of the electorate.

Some candidates may appear to change their message completely as the electorate changes, and in fact, some may completely contradict the earlier message. Be watchful NOT to follow suit, and be prepared, document these changes to use as additional ammunition for your possible negative campaign (See section on campaign ethics and negative campaigning).

It is also important to assure that voters within this narrow demographic feel a specific connection to the candidate. In primary elections, all candidates share a single party affiliation and this negates the fact that candidates and voters have this affiliation in common. For this reason, it is imperative that a candidate make other connections between himself and the voters. This connection can be a personal one based on socio-economic status, family or marital status, age, ethnicity or professional background. Since this an important part of the campaign, it is important early in the planning stages of the race to identify the target electorate by partisanship, geographic area as well as any other threads of commonality that can be identified.

It is particularly important to identify the electorate as a part of planning to spend campaign resources. Typically nearly one half of those who can vote are not registered to do so. Of those registered, another 40 percent often do not participate in a given election. In a primary election, only one half of those left may be registered to your party. This means that of all of the people in a given geographic area, only about 15 percent can and will vote in a primary election. That number grows to more than 30 percent in a general election. There are selected exceptions to this formula, but as a campaign moves ahead, this is a good way to remain focused on identifying and targeting the specific portions of the electorate that can/will respond.

Voter Lists

One of a campaign's most valuable resources is a list of registered voters. These are compiled by county supervisors of elections or boards of elections, and they are available for candidates on computer disk or online as applicable. These lists can be used for many purposes including walk lists, phone lists and to prioritize precincts.

The most common voter lists used by candidates throughout the country come from local elections officials. As the campaign begins contact county supervisors or boards of elections in each, county that is affected by the campaign. Some localities or states make voter data available through a registrar's office. All campaigns should request voter files (voter lists) that are needed as early in the campaign as possible in order to produce:

- Absentee voters lists
- All registered voters in district or county (as needed)
- Make needed payment arrangements: Pay per request or set up accounts if available.

- Newly Registered voters are other good targets.

An additional resource for voter information lists is a candidate's political party. Campaigns should contact their local, state or national party organizations to request or purchase partisan specific lists and software. There may be a fee for this service or a charge for the software.

Some of the most common uses for voter lists are walk lists and phone lists, but lists will be used for a variety of campaign activities.

Walk Lists should target voters that you want to influence. Primary walks may focus on past primary partisan voters, while general election walks may target "swing voters," or those who do not ordinarily vote, vote independently (Reg. Ind. Voters), or democrats who do not typically turn out.

Phone lists for follow-up calls after precinct walks or identify likely supporters (Voter I.D. Calls). Phone lists can also help make certain that supporters vote (for making GOTV calls). Primary Voter I.D. calls should concentrate on precincts with higher turn out, and target partisan voters likely to turn out based on past performance. Primary (GOTV) calls should target supporters identified from earlier calls.

For any, and for all campaign activities, lists will be generated. It is an important tool for tracking voters, volunteers and staff.

Volunteer lists will be generated and used to track all those who volunteer for the campaign. A number of computer software developers have created programs to assist in many campaign tasks. There are many computer programs that have a superb function for volunteer tracking.

Sign lists can also be useful in keeping track of the campaigns many sign locations as well as planning by identifying the contacts made for placing signs.

Generating and using lists is a key part of planning a campaign, particularly when identifying the electorate, and using volunteers.

Ballot Access

Despite a candidate's motivation, as in all things, there must be a beginning. Before a candidate can appeal to voters in a given area, he or she must first make sure that their name is going to appear on the ballot during the election. Simply saying one is running for office does not make it so.

While the methods by which candidates for public office gain access to the ballot vary from state to state and from city to city, there are some common requirements, and some simple steps to making sure your candidate's hard work is tested by the electorate. In almost all cases the simplest way to assure a candidate appears on the ballot is to pay an entrance or qualifying fee. Candidates in many areas throughout the country can also elect to collect petition signatures to gain ballot access, and in some areas a combination of these is required.

Regardless of the chosen method, assuring that your candidate is one of the choices voters see on Election Day is a paramount first step in campaigning.

The first, and arguably simplest, way to ensure a candidate's inclusion is by paying a fee. While fees vary widely, they are regularly based on the salary of a selected office. Part-time municipal offices may require small fees of as little as $25, while state and federal offices can require a much more significant fee in the thousands of dollars. Typically, qualifying or filing fees for higher office are between 1 and 10 percent of the annual salary of the office. While paying these fees is the simplest way to gain ballot access, it is not always the most cost effective or even the most beneficial to the campaign.

Another way candidates can have their names included on the ballot is to collect a set number of petition signatures from within the area affected by the election. The number of signatures required depends largely on the office a candidate is seeking. Smaller county or city races will require fewer signatures than state of federal offices. Some town offices may only require a handful of petitions, as few as 50, while a state legislative race may require more than 2,000 signatures to assure a candidate is listed on the ballot.

There are some advantages to gaining ballot access through petition drives. Chief among these is the ability of the campaign to introduce a candidate to the electorate far in advance of regular campaigning. To ensure that this tactic is successful, the campaign team must always remember that the primary objective is to place the name of their candidate on the Election Day ballot. Unlike other petitions collected by many community activists, a political petition drive requires a few very specific information is gathered. The first is a proper state approved petition form. These forms are typically available at local or state elections offices and are increasingly available on the Internet. Once the proper forms are obtained, some areas require that a campaign announce its intent to qualify for the election by petition drive. In most cases, petition signatures may only be obtained from registered voters within the boundaries of the district, county or city. Petitions drives for partisan offices or primary elections may also require that signatories be of the same party affiliation as the candidate, or at the least of the party whose nomination is being sought.

The two most common ways to collect petitions are through the campaigns door-to-door walking campaign or as an additional early campaign mail program. Both are affected and give the candidate a chance to appear in some form in front of likely voters at least once in advance of the traditional campaigning period. By approaching voters in this way and requesting assistance in putting a candidate's name on the ballot the campaign is engaging a select portion of the electorate. This can give the candidate a chance to make an impression on voters, which makes the petition drive an excellent chance to promote the candidate. It is important to remember that this can also be hazardous if candidates aren't yet prepared to answer questions, engage strangers or prepare a proper walk or mailing list.

In some smaller districts or city elections, candidates may be required to pay a filing fee and collect petitions to qualify for the ballot. Early in the planning stages of the campaign, staff should thoroughly research the methods of obtaining ballot access, and once a method is selected, make it a primary objective of early

campaigning. To begin, campaign staff should contact local or state

elections officials as early as possible.

G.W. Pomichter

Petition Collection Checklist

1. Research: most populated precincts   _____

a. Use past election results

2. Research petition signatory requirements   _____

3. Print approved petition forms   _____

4. Research: Target Voters   _____

5. Print Walk Lists and Maps   _____

6. Separate Walk Lists

a. Walk-able areas in Targeted Precincts   _____

b. Even Side of Road   _____

c. Odd Side of Road   _____

7. Create Walk Script

a. Greeting   _____

b. Required petition   _____

c. Candidate info.   _____

8. Choose Walk or Mail plan   _____

9. Set Walk Date/Mail Drop Date   _____

10. Organize Volunteers:

a. Call Walkers from Volunteer list   _____

b. Call Organizations to get volunteers   _____

c. Keep a list of those who commit to walk   _____

d. Follow-up with walkers to confirm   _____

e. Follow Walk-Checklist   _____

G.W. Pomichter

Campaign Budgeting

As in any business or household venture, it is crucial that a political campaign establish a working budget under which to operate. This budget should identify each specific cost associated with the campaign

Since a political campaign is not driven by the sale of a specific tangible product or service, the budget for a campaign will focus almost exclusively on expenditures, with the understanding that the money spent will have to be generated by the campaign's fund raising efforts.

For the purposes of budgeting, the campaign is an exercise in marketing. It will identify specific advertising media and show planned expenses in order of priority. For example a primary election's budget may place little emphasis on television or newspaper advertising, and significant emphasis on targeted direct mail.

In addition to these major costs, the campaign budget should include one-time or incidental expenses such as business card printing, signs and paid staff to assist in developing a volunteer team.

In many races, outside expert consultants may be required to assist in the strategic development of the campaign. These represent another cost, and should be included in preparing a campaign budget.

A separate budget should be established for each election in which a candidate is expected to participate. For example, a campaign should prepare a budget for a primary election, and then a separate budget for the general election. It is not advisable to plan to use a single budget for both elections, as both expenditures and funding source availability will change after each victory.

Once a budget is established, it is imperative that the campaign focus its fundraising efforts on raising no less than the budgeted minimum. Additional funds can be used for enhancing the campaign, but it is difficult to overcome core budget shortfalls.

The campaign budget is a living document and will change as your strategy evolves.

G.W. Pomichter

SAMPLE ONLY

Campaign BUDGET

Opening (Name I.D.) POLL:		**11,417**		2,500.00
Mail Plan				
To Primary Election Super Voters:		**11,417**		
To Win 50%+1 =			**5,710**	
Petition Drive Biographical Information:	ALL		5,138.00	
Return Postage 1/2			2,055.00	
Palm cards		**10,000**		3,500.00
Introduction Mailer:	ALL			5,138.00
Issues Mailer 1:		ALL		5,138.00
Issue 2		ALL		5,138.00
Issue 3		ALL		5,138.00
Pre - POLL				2,500.00
"Spouse" Piece:	Women:		**7300+/-**	3,492.00
Attack1	ALL	**11,417**		5,138.00
Push Poll	ALL	**11,417**		1,500.00
Attack2	Neg-Only	**5,000+/-**		2,250.00
3. GOTV Mailer: Election Date		**5,710+/-**		2,570.00
Reminder to Vote				
Voter for (The candidate)				
Absentee Mailer	By-REQ	**8000+/-**		3,900.00
Signage				
1. Commercial Signs 200 Qt.				4,000.00
2. Yard Signs 1000 Qt.				3,000.00
Radio Plan 1. Production:				1,500.00
a. Intro spot: Bio/Resume				1,000.00
b. Issues: GOTV				1,000.00
Staff:			4 (x) 2,000	8,000.00
Office Supplies:				5,000.00
Misc. Print Ads				9,000.00
Consult:			(x) 2	25,000.00
Min. TOTAL:				$112,596.00

G.W. Pomichter

The Candidate

The candidate has **5** primary responsibilities during the campign:

1.   Raise money

2.   Meet voters

3.   Motivate volunteers

4.   Speaking arrangements and forums

5.   Final approval of all campaign communications (Paid and

Free)

Raise Money

Bottom line, a campaign cannot win on door-to-door efforts alone. Considering the quality of the opposition and the potential for an even larger field every penny designated in the budget will be necessary. If the campaign is to be successful in reaching the fundraising goals, you must be personally engaged on a daily basis. The schedule should allocate three hours every day to make either fundraising visits or phone calls.

Meet Voters

The most important asset the campaign possesses is the drive and work ethic of the candidate. When all is said and done - you will win over voters one-by-one, house-by-house, street-by-street, and neighborhood-by-neighborhood. Advertising is important in a vacuum but it will never replace the personal touch - a candidate asking for a voter's trust and their vote. Beginning in mid-August, the Campaign Coordinator should keep you on a schedule to personally visit 500 homes per week.

Motivating Volunteers

Beginning almost immediately, the campaign should host weekly or biweekly volunteer appreciation parties. Every volunteer should receive a phone call from the candidate once a week to solicit campaign advice and intelligence from them.

Speaking Engagements and Forums

These shows are a necessary evil of campaigning. Unfortunately, you will talk to the same handful of activists in every meeting. Your goal is not to say or do anything stupid that an opponent can use against us in the future.

Final Approval of All Campaign Communications

The operational words for the campaign are "final" and "approval". This should not degenerate into rewriting and designing material in an effort to avoid raising money, recruiting and motivating volunteers and talking to voters. Someone other than the candidate should perform these initial tasks. The candidate cannot get involved in organizing the schedule, supervising all volunteers, writing press releases, designing direct mail or placing out signs. These tasks would become all-consuming and the real work of the candidate would not get done.

Fund Raising

One of the most critical parts of the campaign is raising funds needed to get the campaign message to the voters. There are many types of fund raising activities, but the most common are "events" and direct solicitation by the candidate.

While fundraising events offer an opportunity for contributors to meet face-to-face with the candidate, it is also the most logistically challenging.

The most important part of planning a fund raising event is securing the sponsors of the event. These are contributors who make large maximum allowable contributions and pledge to collect a specific amount from those who they know, whether or not they actually attend the event. This includes the host of the event. Campaign staffers should be sure to keep an accurate list of event sponsors and note what amount each has pledged to collect

Ideally, the host of such an event will be responsible for securing sponsors, developing the invitation lists, and planning the event. In some instances however, the campaign staff will be asked to fill some of these logistical responsibilities, such as printing and mailing invitations, or securing facilities. Remember, as the campaign progresses the amount of logistical support that the campaign staff can provide for each event will become limited by time constraints.

In cases where the hosts produce and mail invitations the appropriate disclaimer will apply on all printed materials. This may read similarly to this: "pd. pol. adv. paid for by (host) approved by (candidate) (R or party)." ALL In kind contributions are limited to the maximum allowed by state law for each contributor (sponsor or host). All contributions are limited by state law per contributor. Campaigns should be keenly aware of state and federal laws governing such disclaimers for the office sought. If the invitation is printed, mailed and paid for by the campaign the appropriate political ad. Disclaimer will apply. This will read: "pd. pol. adv. paid for by (campaign) approved by (candidate) (D or R)." This disclaimer will differ from state to state and may require specific language so it important to research the state-specific requirements.

Any amount paid by the host for facilities, refreshments, food, invitations, or other expense associated with an event must be claimed by the campaign as an in-kind contribution. For this reason receipts and an EXACT accounting of these incidental expenses are crucial.

If the candidate is expected to speak (formally) at the event the host and campaign staff should:

1.   Provide an appropriate (approved) introduction of the candidate.

2.   Provide Biographical information about the candidate.

3.   Provide the candidate with information about the audience, guests or group to be addressed.

At the event one person should be designated to be responsible for "holding" checks that are received so that processing these will be less confusing. The fewer people "holding" money means fewer chances for losses or errors. Remember that some contributors will give checks directly to staffers or candidates at events. Always inform the candidate of money received by others at an event.

Track event specific contributions that are received before, during and after the event. This will help to establish which events were the most beneficial to the campaign.

An accurate map and good directions to events should be researched and printed for The candidate and for any guests that may call and need these details.

Staff should arrive at least 30 minutes prior to any event to prepare name badges, set up check-in tables or make last minute preparations for the candidate before his arrival. At any event the campaign should be able to see how well the event was attended and by whom. To this end, a sign in station (table) should be set up and a sign-in sheet should be maintained. Name badges (shirt size) are also a must for most events: be sure to have these ordered before any fundraising event. Using a guest check-in list of those invited will expedite this process when such a list is available. When a "fill-in-the-blanks" type list is used it should include space for the full names and mailing addresses of all those who attended in case follow-up letters or thank you cards are to be sent.

Checks from an event must be processed as soon as possible. (See "Processing funds"). Make sure information about contributors is complete for reporting purposes.

There are many ways of soliciting funds from likely contributors. All of these will require research and prior planning. The most effective fund raising resource on the team is The candidate. The candidate is the only person on the team who should solicit funds, unless he or she authorizes someone else to do so.

Research is an essential part of fundraising. Identifying likely contributors is critical to the solicitation process. Knowing where to look is vital to the campaign's success. Past contributors to similar campaigns are a good place start. Business leaders who are familiar with The candidate may be another valuable source of funding. Those who have contributed to candidates of the same party are also likely to support The candidate financially as are lobbyists and organizations that have like-minded agendas as The candidate's.

Making contact with those on your "likely contributors" list can be done in a few ways. A direct phone call from the candidate will likely yield the best results. A letter from the candidate requesting support can also be an effective fundraising tool.

A letter from the campaign soliciting support is not the most desirable way to solicit funds, as it is the least personal, but it has been used effectively by some campaigns.

Once the campaign has decided which of these fundraising techniques to use, some thought should be given to how to handle contributions as they are received. Funds should be processed as they arrive. Here are rules for receiving these funds.

✓ Always inform the candidate of who has sent money. This will avoid calling a second time (which is redundant and can be embarrassing).

✓ Note who contributed funds AND who may have solicited the funds (i.e. lobbyists, organizations etc…)

It is important to keep complete records of campaign contributors. A campaign requires (by law) precise records of all financial transactions. For this reason, the method by which you process and maintain records of contributions is very important.

✓   Each contributor may only contribute a limited amount. In Florida for example, $500.00 per election/campaign cycle (Federal campaigns differ).

✓   Verify that each contributor has not exceeded the state's statutory limit.

Ideally, make copies of this information so that one copy will be given to treasurer for entry into reporting software or on reporting documents. For ease and convenience, a staff member may be elected to enter contribution data into and work with the treasurer on reports. If this is the case, only one person should be charged with this responsibility to avoid confusion. Since this information is for reporting purposes, it should be as detailed as possible.

Remember for ALL contributions, the occupation of the contributor should be recorded. A copy should be used to enter data into a database for use producing "thank you" letters; then, this copy should be filed with a copy of the specific deposit slip in a Master list of contributors organized by deposit, date and number. Another copy may be attached to a "thank you" letter to help the candidate recall the detail of the contributor.

Thank you letters or cards ensure that contributors know that the campaign is grateful for their support. Producing these letters is an important part of the processing of funds. Enter check information in to a thank you database. While some reporting software will produce a generic thank you letter, the use of a separate database will allow a more customized and more "individually" appropriate letter to be produced. Once letters are printed, place with prepared envelope attached to copy of check and accompanying information and send to candidate for signature or correction. Make corrections to letters in a timely manner.

Once letters are signed make courtesy copies, as well as a copy of the letter for the office file, and mail.

Once contributions are processed funds should be deposited as soon as possible. By statute, in Florida for example the campaign has ten days in which to deposit funds received; it is however, a good practice to make deposits daily to avoid confusion.

Contribution Processing Check List

1. Contribution Received and amount can be accepted _____

2. Contributors occupation _____

3. Contribution and accompanying materials copied

a. for treasurer _____

b. for Master file and thank you database _____

c. for candidate with thank you letter _____

4. Contribution entered in Reporting Software _____

5. Contribution added to "daily" deposit slip _____

6. Contributor added to thank you database _____

7. Thank you letter printed with accompanying envelope _____

8. Thank you, envelopes and copies sent to candidate for signature _____

9. Deposit slip closed at the end of EACH day _____

a. Deposits MUST be made within 10 (Ten) days of receipt.

10. Deposit slip copied:

a. for treasurer's file _____

b. for Master file _____

c. for security file _____

11. Deposit funds (Call bank for pick up) _____

   a. *No cash can be sent by bank courier... must be deposited directly.*

G.W. Pomichter

Advertising

Perhaps the most important part of any campaign is getting the campaign's message to the voters. For this reason, the weapons in the campaign arsenal are varied, but all are likely forms of advertising. Like any product or service, advertising is key to this goal. Unlike a permanent business, a political campaign must sell its product, the candidate, in a distinctly short and well-defined period. For this reason, identifying the likely customers and effectively targeting this limited portion of the consumer public is vital.

Most people are familiar with the most common types of advertising, but with a limited target market and a short period of time to achieve the requisite 50 percent plus one market share, it is crucial to prioritize advertising according to its ability to reach very select groups with very specific message segments.

Another critical concern of campaign advertising must be the limited amount of time that is available for voters to respond to messages they receive from campaigns. Unlike other products or services, voters may only choose a candidate on Election Day. Some areas have early voting and some voters can vote using absentee ballots, but all options limit the time that a candidate can secure the 50 percent plus one vote needed to win.

Print advertising such as advertisements in newspaper or targeted periodicals are one way of delivering the campaign message to large numbers of likely voters. Similarly targeted event programs (Republican or Democratic Picnic flyers) and billboards can be investments that can pay off with a limited response from voters.

A campaign's signs are often the most visible media used in a political campaign. Commercial signs and residential yard signs are commonly considered a necessary purchase by any campaign at any level of government.

Mass media such as radio or television and the blossoming internet are most often thought to be the best way to reach the largest audience. While this is true, since the campaign has a specific and extremely narrow focus, its use of mass media outlets should be decided on a case-by-case basis with the guiding principals being cost effectiveness and consideration for the size of the targeted audience.

Targeted direct mailers are another medium that campaigns have traditionally made good use. These can be used to deliver the campaign message while collecting petitions, introduce the candidate to the voters, contact absentee voters or encourage voters to participate in the election as in the case of GOTV mailers.

In a traditional business venture time and a graduated consistency of message can be achieved through short blasts of advertising in selected mediums such as television or radio. Direct mail is often discounted for its costs proportionate to the immediate or long tern responses it generates. Most marketing studies indicate that direct mail affectively delivers a message for about 7 seconds once it is received. For this reason, as well as the limited repetition of images, symbols and specific psychological language, this medium is often disregarded in favor of television or other mass media.

In a political campaign, however, direct mail has the ability to target a candidate's message to a specific and limited demographic. Since the target audience is narrower than with many products, and since messages can both inspire positive and negative responses to a candidate, more focused methods can yield the best results.

For this reason, direct mail is widely considered the best medium for campaign advertising. Radio, television, commercial and residential signs as well as other media can be affectively used as tools for reinforcing messages initially delivered through this medium.

When evaluating various media, there a several things to consider. When choosing media, choose most targetable media first, such as direct mailers, periodicals (The Local Happenings), newspapers by zip code or niche" radio stations.

Mass media may be likewise evaluated by considering its audience as well. Television, for example, is one of the most pervasive advertising mediums, but in a political campaign is the least target able. This media, if properly used, however can result is high name recognition. The costs associated with television advertising make it less cost effective for smaller races with narrower voter targets.

Research is another crucial part of planning a campaign's advertising. Campaign staffers should research publishing or airing schedules for local or targeted media outlets. In order to plan, the campaign will also have to research pricing for each media to be used. It is important that prices include copy or production costs. Demographic research will help to target advertising viewers who are part or the entire targeted voter block.

✓ Which geographic areas are covered by a medium?

✓ Who will be reached by the message?

The campaign should have marked maps of municipality, county, or district as well as comparable media coverage areas,

Prices and distribution information should be kept available throughout the campaign for the candidate's consideration.

Cautions

1. Proof read all ads and save a copy of proof for files.

2. Misspellings are common mistakes. It is especially vital to ensure that names of people and locations are spelled correctly.

3. Photos should be crisp and clear or they should not be used.

4. All ads should be cost effective. All advertisers believe in their medium, so let the campaign decide what is most effective.

5. All advertising MUST contain appropriate disclaimers.

Campaign Mail Plans

Direct mail is the most targetable for of campaign advertising. For this reason it is the most used. Because this will be one of the campaign's most critical resources it seems prudent to spend a moment examining the elements of a well though out mail plan. There are several strategies for direct mail, but all seem to consist of some basic psychological elements. Since the purpose of any advertising in the campaign is to giver voters a reason to support a candidate and to give then their vote, a mail plan must address one of, or all of the fundamental reasons people will vote: Sentiment, Commonality, or trust. A traditional mail plan consists of all three of these elements in varying degrees.

65

Sentiment:

A traditional mail plan will include introduction and biographical material as one of the candidate's first mail pieces. It is important that recipients of the piece get a sense of who the candidate is, and where they come from. There are a couple of ways to accomplish this.

Smaller campaigns may choose to reserve their resources and introduce their candidate by telling both their personal and professional stories in a single mailer. This should include the candidate's upbringing, education, their family life, marital status, professional resume, and personal philosophy. These are elements that help to establish a sense that the reader is getting to know your candidate, and building a slight sentimental connection to them.

Larger campaigns with greater financial resources should consider breaking this introduction into smaller parts and sending separate mailers. This is because the sentimental illusion will be stronger if the information takes more of a period of time. These mailers should begin with the personal introduction with information about the life, family and personal goals and philosophies of the candidate. This will establish a feeling of familiarity with them. The next phase of this strategy is to send the professional history of the candidate which will include a kind of professional resume, and mentions of any political experience the campaign deems relevant. By receiving these separately, voters may perceive a more lasting bond forming, and the sentiment factor on Election Day is stronger.

Commonality:

A select but vital group of voters choose candidates much more carefully, based on the perception that a candidate has a common view of issues? These more informed voters want to know that a candidate is on their side. Mailers showing that your candidate's views are important. This may also be achieved through single or multiple mail pieces.

Smaller campaigns may elect a single mail piece containing positions on multiple issues. It is strongly recommended that a mailer of this type be limited to and include three issues and your candidate's position on each. This will not overload the reader, but will give them a well-rounded look at the top policy opinions of your candidate. Remember that most people receive dozens of mailers and have a limited amount of time to spend on your so keep it direct and short.

Larger campaigns should focus each mailer on a single issue. This will give the more studious voter a more in depth look at The candidate and the less anxious will at minimum receive The candidate 's name to look at multiple times. When organizing these issue mailers, identify the most important three issues in an area or race and send a single mailer addressing each. Again, the long term nature of this promotes the perception of many conversations with the candidate and an impression that a voter is more informed about the candidate.

Trust:

The final phase of the mail plan is to establish trust about the election with each recipient. By encouraging them to vote, you illustrate that you trust their judgment, and ask them once more for their support. This is also the phase where candidates may choose to distinguish themselves from their opponents.

"Niche" Mailers and Endorsements:

The endorsement list should include present and past elected or respected officials, present and past city elected, Republican executive committee members, club presidents, precinct officials, chamber officials, activist groups (party groups, environmental groups, police unions, firefighters, economic development council members, homeowner groups, women's groups, etc.), owners and/or managers of major employers and local media professionals.

Finally, the campaign will implement a strategy to identify sympathetic and structured interest groups with whom endorsements will resonate, and develop specific niche mini-campaigns for each group. Niche groups might include: Attorneys and their families and employees, elder voters and their families, police and their families, firefighters and their families, teachers and their families, tea party groups, and homeowners groups.

Customize:

The smaller city or county race may send only one piece, asking voters to remember when Election Day is, and comparing themselves and their opponents so that voters have this comparison at the polls. It is important to be careful when attempting this combination. Voters must get the message that you trust them, so that they will trust you. Larger campaigns that break this message up can attack opponents when necessary, but those smaller campaigns walk a finer line, and should focus strictly on comparisons and reminder to vote. Let the voter do the rest of the work.

Larger campaigns again have an advantage here. They often can afford tracking polls to keep them closely abreast of the ebbs and flows of their campaign. That allows them to most effectively send a comparison mailer followed by attack mailers when needed, and finishing with the reminder to vote, and the request of support. This strategy allows voters to build trust over several mailers, and this trust is based more effectively on what is perceived by the willingness of your candidate to share a significant amount of information, as long as that information remains accurate.

Good mail plans will focus a campaign message using all three of these elements, and will include a minimum of three direct mail pieces. Regardless of your budget, or the size of your district direct mail will play a significant roll in your campaign, and should be used to communicate the most focused message that your candidate should be elected. Sentimentality, Commonality and Trust are your goals with direct mail, and the incidental benefit that results from your attempts to establish these is increased name identification. If used effectively even a plan that only establishes one or a portion of the psychological elements may see a dramatic rise in name I.D. that could be beneficial on Election Day.

G.W. Pomichter

The Internet & Social Media

While many experts struggle with the emerging uses of internet, smart phone and social media technologies, the impact of these rapidly developing and changing media cannot be simply ignored. The results of aggressive social media and internet campaigning have yet to be fully quantified. Some long time campaign managers and directors believe that the impact of such campaigns is negligible, while others believe they have played vital rolls in victory.

One thing is certain, and that is that web based campaigning has become a part of the classic campaign strategy, and that if employed as a part of the greater campaign plan, it has benefits and pitfalls of which campaigns should be aware.

A major benefit of social media and internet based campaign elements is repetition and coverage. Internet sites, Facebook pages, Twitter accounts and e-mails help a candidate to establish a constant presence in the lives of potential voters, and can, if employed correctly, provide repeated exposure to the campaign message.

Contrarily, this constant exposure to a broad audience can result in increased scrutiny of the campaign's message, and to the candidate who will be the presumed author of all internet and social media content.

Another pitfall of aggressive social media campaigns is over exposure for a candidate. The more a candidate engages an audience, the greater the likelihood that a mistake will be made or a comment can be misunderstood. The key to avoiding these missteps is constant editorial review and specifically designated campaign staff to direct and steer the web based efforts.

Once a staff member or volunteer has been tasked with a candidate's "social media" campaign, messaging will be an important part of their functions. Every web or social media post should receive the same scrutiny that a press release or paid advertisements receives. It should be edited, challenged for understandability and, of course, be grammatically correct. Since social media should be used as a compliment to other forms of communication, each and all social posts should be consistent with the campaign's over-all message. Issue statements should be clear, short and engaging, but should also be in complete and unmistakable agreement with published and stated beliefs of the candidate. Care should be taken to ensure that a post to a blog or social media site, while remaining as "social" as possible, cannot be taken as a contradiction of a candidate's policy or social beliefs as will be later or may have been earlier stated.

It is further important to remember that a social media site is in fact a "public" forum. For this reason it is particularly important not to engage in arguments or disagreements openly while engaging social media. Periodically, social media followers will voice disagreements with a candidate's posted opinions or policy questions. In many online and social media circles, those who continuously seek out controversy or "confrontation" are called "trolls." These should be a concern to any Campaign member assisting with social media, and should be avoided when possible. Great care should be taken not to engage in "back-and-forth" discussions, as tempers and egos may cause supporters and staffers as well as the candidate to become defensive and increase the chances of making inappropriate or easily misinterpreted statements.

It is important also to remember that a key element of smaller, district and municipal level campaigns is targeting. Social media, internet presence and web blogs are all very generally distributed to a broad, often global audience, and while this may have some advantages in establishing image, the limited impact of a global presence within a limited geographic area should not be overestimated. If, for example, a candidate boasts 5,000 Facebook ™ friends, it is highly unlikely that a large proportion of these will be eligible to vote in the election. This being the case, a campaign can neither rely upon social media successes as a gauge for the overall campaign success, nor gauge an opponent based on their social media presence. It is important to remember to be especially cautious of engaging in "back-and-forth debates with opposition campaigns in this medium.

Another critical online pitfall to avoid is "testing the waters." Do not use social media as a petri dish for testing messages. It is vital to remember that once a statement or message is posted to an internet site, it can never be fully retracted or controlled. Copying mistakes from a candidate's social media presence has become a prolific part of negative campaigning.

As the technology evolves, greater access to voter e-mails, cellular phone numbers and web data may become available, and with this information, web based and social media campaign elements may become more easily targetable, and have greater effectiveness. For this reason, campaigns should remain aware of advances in the technology that can benefit candidates.

It is vital that just as with any other media employed by the campaign, social media, web pages, blogs and e-mail, be used as a singular part of the larger campaign. These tools are only as effective as their employment as part of the greater campaign tools candidates utilize.

G.W. Pomichter

Absentee Ballot Mail Program

The absentee ballot program has always been extremely important, but has become increasingly significant in recent years because "anyone" can apply for an absentee ballot, even if one will not be actually absent. Because any eligible voter can now cast their vote from the comfort of their own home in many states, contact with these voters is crucial and can indeed swing an election.

The campaign should begin by making a list of the counties or portions of counties the office sought will represent, and make contact with county or local elections officials.

    a. Get to know their rules for payments and pickup of absentee lists

b. Get the name of a consistent contact person in each office

c. Get mailing information such as when is the first drop, when will absentee names be available after initial pick up.

d. Fill out paper work / include all the names of people picking up labels

e. Start a bank account if applicable

f. Confirm a schedule of "drops" by finding a reliable volunteer/supporter who is available "regularly."

g. Assign someone to pick up labels in county daily, every other day, etc…

h. Be sure they know the rules for their assigned county

i. Be sure they will be at the Elections office first thing in the morning

Use disk to make labels to send absentee Mailer or if available, from the supervisor's or Board of Elections office, campaigns may elect to receive labels pre-printed.

Pre-printed labels allow a volunteer to work almost exclusively from home if they choose. (Be sure to have a copy of these pre-printed labels made for chaser calls…)

Write an appropriate script for persuasive chaser calls

Some examples are:

- o "Soon you will be receiving your absentee ballot…"

- o "May I tell you about my friend (candidate)…?"

- o "By now you should have received your absentee ballots…"

✓ Organize volunteers to start phone banks.

Arrange a phone bank to start calling before the first "drop" is made by Supervisor of Elections office.

Continue these phone bank schedules until you receive negative responses

By election time constituents are bombarded with candidate solicitations, it is a good idea to gauge your progress and not become the one that turns a voter "off."

Photocopy the label list

Label the mailer pieces and mail immediately

Use the copy to find phone numbers

Keep a file for each county's labels, phone numbers and

general information.

<u>Signs</u>

Sign Design & Color Selection

Designing campaign signs is a precise business that encompasses among many things budgeting, personal preferences of candidates and a fundamental understanding of the psychology of colors.

The campaign's budget can limit sign color choices because printing costs often vary based upon the number of colors being used on a sign. In the case of budget, if your campaign is choosing to go one-color for letters or one for the background, options are limited. Candidates might like the idea of using exaggerated colors such as purple to express knowledge, but depending upon the shade which might require mixing more than one color; this may not be the best used of funds upon a singular standard background color.

While many candidates like to select patriotic colors to convey their desire to serve in government, it is not highly recommended, especially if there are numerous other campaigns doing the same. It's can be very difficult to draw the attention of voters to your sign, without producing signs that looks markedly similar to a large number of other candidates seeking elected offices in your geographic area or district.

Once your team has considered these factors, it will be time to consider the campaign's message and the best colors to convey it psychologically. Black, for example, conveys power and authority and can be easy to see from the road. In contrast, white is a reasonable background color, but it's associations with cleanliness and desolation are not particularly meaningful to voters. Red is a color that typically means power or intellect, but also has strong connections with love, while blue is a freshening and calming color that may temper voters angry with government.

Other colors that some campaigns pass over with little consideration, but that are worthy of note include green, which is a symbol of the natural world and may connect a candidate with environmental issues, or yellow, which conveys a bright and cheery disposition, especially when paired with a dark contrasting color. Purple, as previously noted, conveys wisdom, but also royalty and leadership, but is perhaps too evocative of royalty to be used by "grassroots campaigns."

Rarely do campaigns consider using brown, which like green, is an earth tone has been shown by psychologists to evoke in people images of the environment. Orange is another often overlooked color that conveys excitement, warmth, and is additionally very bright andgarners attention well.

It is fair to say, that campaign managers, consultants and even sign designers have many differing points of view about the role that color plays when used on campaign signs. Some voters are more influenced by color than others and depending upon someone's temperament and their disposition emotional responses to color will be different. For this reason, campaign signs should effectively communicate a candidate's presence and perform a function of increasing the visibility of a candidate's name above any other consideration.

Commercial Signs: Commercial signs are an important part of the over-all campaign plan. Their placement and planning can increase name I.D. and visibility. The proper use of these can also promote an image of success and ever-presence.

The first step in planning for your commercial sign placement is to develop a placement plan. Determine the most desirable locations for commercial signs. High Traffic areas will yield the best results. When information is available, using actual traffic data collected by state and local governments is best. Do not rely upon a "best guess."

The campaign may also select key parts of the district with low (or NO name I.D.), or parts where there is a high concentration of voters (using precinct performance data) are the best locations for signs.

Next, contact business and property owners. Local real estate companies for example often have lists of properties they manage or are responsible for selling. Pay particular attention to large commercial lots located on busy roads and intersections. Contact businesses on major roads or at busy intersections.

It is important to get signed authorizations with drawn maps from owners or managers of these properties. Be sure to use these locations or contact the owners or managers if you will not be using them. People who support the candidate and offer sign locations like to know that they are a part of the campaign.

Again, research is important. Knowing city and county Ordinances about political signs will save the campaign from costly mistakes and possible fines. Some cities or counties require a permit, fee or deposit to place signs of a specific size. Paying these fees or deposits and filing any forms needed in cities and counties will protect the candidate and the campaign and insure that campaign money is not wasted on unnecessary fines or penalties. Some areas also have time restrictions about "when" you may place signs, such as 90 days prior to the election, etc… knowing these time restrictions is essential to getting prime location as early as possible.

The campaign should be sure to get accurate count of signs "on-hand" or order signs to meet the need of the placement plan. (Make sure you have some "extra" for repairs or for locations that become available after the placement plan is met.) Check supplies of support poles, and other periphery needed to install signs.

With Authorizations, and permits acquired schedule placement crews. Solicit help from volunteers to:

✓   To assemble.

✓   To Place.

The campaign may also consider calling on organizations with specific knowledge of the area or district such as police or firefighters.

It is also important to make sure that crews have the proper tools to work with such as battery powered screw drivers (drills), post-hole diggers. A small truck may also be needed to carry signs.

The campaign should maintain an accurate list of signs and locations that are placed, and those that need to be. Once signs are placed, they may require maintenance to keep them in good repair.

Once signs are initially placed, consider enhancements that may be helpful.

➤ "Thank you" signs

➤ "Vote Today" signs

➤ Special signs

"Thank you „Candidate" for…" (Project name), these give residents of specific areas a way to relate to an experienced candidate.

Sign Removal: There are required time limits on the removal of signs from specific cities, and time requirements vary. Check your ordinances and remove signs in a timely manner. The campaign should get volunteer placement crews to remove signs that they placed.

Residential (Yard Signs): Residential signs can be a valuable way to display the support of the community. They also have a limited value in lower traffic areas not covered by your commercial sign plan.

One of the most effective deployments of yard signs is at key precincts on Election Day. In fact, all polling places where voters may vote for the candidate.

89

1.   Get an accurate count of precincts (polling places) in the district.

2.   Count all existing signs, (OR) order yard signs in a quantity that is adequate to put at least one at every precinct (polling place) and give several to supporters who wish to display them in their yards.

It is important to the campaign to keep an up-to-date list of all supporters who request yard signs and how many they have. These signs CAN be used again and we will need to get them back after the campaign is over. Keep a record of yard signs that are placed by campaign staff on intersections and on roads.

One pit fall the campaign should avoid is becoming one of a "bunch" on what have been called "sign farms" where every other candidate has placed their yard signs. These locations become overcrowded and signs become a "blur" to the passing traffic.

Some municipalities also require the same permitting or application fees for small signs as for large, when placed. Researching these requirements is a campaign must.

Staff should avoid placing signs in the public "rights-of-way," this is illegal as it may cause accidents and can result in signs being removed by county or city authorities. A good rule-of-thumb is to use the telephone poles on a street as a guide (these are placed on their own right-of-way, and not on public rights-of way).

Sign installers list

_____ Sign message panels: Endorsements/Election Days/Thank You

_____ Steaks

_____ Post hold diggers

_____ Hammer & Nails

_____ Drill, batters charger & screws

_____ Machete, sickle or Weed and Brush remover

_____ Snake bite kit

G.W. Pomichter

Sign Check List

1. Research Local and county ordinances

a. make a list of ALL municipalities in district   _____

b. make a list of all counties in district   _____

c. organize a master list of ALL sign ordinances by County or city   _____

d. research and pay any fees or make deposits as needed   _____

e. keep a running list or fees and deposits made   _____

2. Develop Placement Plans within district   _____

3. Contact all Commercial Real Estate companies

a. Get signed approvals (with maps) for properties controlled or owned   _____

b. Organize list of these properties with maps to locations   _____

4. Contact Business owners with "store fronts."

a. Get signed authorizations for these locations   _____

b. Add locations to master placement list   _____

5. Count all available signs (or) order any needed commercial or yard signs to meet the needs of placement plan.

a. How many commercial signs needed   _____

b. How many commercial signs "on-hand"   _____

c. How many yard signs needed   _____

d. How many yard signs "on-hand"   _____

6. Develop placement teams: Contact volunteers   _____

b. Which volunteers willing to place commercial signs?   _____

c. Have tools/Need tools?   _____

d. contact organizations   _____

e. Which organizations willing to place signs?   _____

f. Have tools/Need tools?   _____

g. Divide locations among teams (geographically is best)   _____

7. Set placement dates

a. When are volunteers available to pick up signs? _____

b. When will organizations be able to pick up signs? _____

8. Follow-up

a. Where are all placed signs? _____

b. Are all locations covered? _____

c. Are there any signs left? _____

d. Are there any more locations to add to plan? _____

9. Placing precinct signs on "election-eve":

a. Who will place which precincts? _____

b. who will remove _____

10. Sign Removal after elections:

a. Have all volunteers who placed signs been called? _____

b. Have all organizations that placed signs been called? _____

c. Who will remove any left-over signs from locations? _____

11. Apply for refunds of deposits and permit fees that apply. _____

Sign Waving Campaign

Another excellent use of political signs is the organized sign waving event. It has been said, "Never let them see you sweat." This motto may have been well use for deodorant commercials, but in campaigns, it does not apply.

THEY LOVE TO SEE YOU SWEAT.

A great way to sweat is standing on a street corner, surrounded if possible by supporters and friends, in the heat and humidity of the day. While It is certainly not the most targeted campaign tactic, it can be said appropriately that sign waving is a necessary evil in campaigns.

By using the voter turnout data, and D.O.T. traffic reports, key intersections that feed into the high turnout precincts should be identified and staffed by wavers.

Beginning as early as volunteers are available and willing, the campaign should systematically cover urban street corners that are highly traveled arteries use by as many of the voters in the district as can be identified. Using campaign signs on stakes, team leaders and volunteers should attempt to wave and make eye contact with as many commuters as possible. The campaign may also elect to use the precinct walk schedule to identify nearby intersections to allow volunteers unable to participate in the walk, to wave for those hours scheduled.

This should present the perception in voter's minds that the candidate is "everywhere" and "really wants their vote," if he or she is willing to try and greet me each morning and afternoon during the rush hour commute.

Volunteer Activities

Volunteers are the heart and soul of any campaign. They help to accomplish a variety of tasks from office work to sign waving and precinct walks. Keeping volunteers busy without exhausting them is a delicate balance that the campaign must find. Some things to remember when working with volunteers are:

1.   While soliciting volunteer help find out what a volunteer is interested in doing for the campaign.

2.   Keep a list of ALL volunteers (with addresses and phone numbers), and keep it up to date with information about what each is willing to do.

3.   When scheduling volunteers make sure that there is work for them. (Bored volunteers will not return when they are "really" needed.)

Activities for Volunteers include preparing "niche'"" or select mailings: (while bulk mail should be more cost effectively done by professional mail houses smaller mailings can and should be done by volunteers.) Volunteers can also research addresses and other information, fold letters and stuff and stamp envelopes

Another popular volunteer activity is running phone banks. Volunteers are vital to making phone calls for a variety of reasons including walk follow-up calls, voter I.D. calls, Get Out The Vote (GOTV) calls and absentee mailer follow-up calls.

Every campaign must also have office help. Volunteers can be helpful in many ways doing day-to-day office work which frees up staff to work on specific projects. Interested volunteers can be helpful answering phones, filing or copying maps, lists or other campaign documents.

REMEMBER: Send thank you notes. Be sure your volunteers know how much the campaign and the candidate appreciates their support. Volunteers are the campaigns most valuable resource. In many campaigns it is easier to raise money than to secure enough volunteer support to run an effective campaign.

Phone Banking

Phone banking, when used effectively, can be an effective and low cost way to reach voters. Like much of a campaign's message delivery, there are some vital elements to successful campaign call strategies. Among the top elements of a volunteer phone bank is personalization, script fluidity and closing.

It is a vital first step to make call personal to the recipient. The campaign should not let the volunteers sound like they're simply reading a script. Each caller needs to be confident and bring a energy and enthusiasm about the candidate to the call. Volunteers should use a voter's proper salutation and name when speaking to them and must speak clearly articulating the approved campaign message with ease. The staff must be sure the script sounds conversational and covers all of the information voters need.

Next, it is vital that callers remain "on message" with their calls to voters. For this reason and the comfort of volunteers, even the most experienced volunteers will perform better with a good well-crafted script. Prior to making calls, each volunteer should practice the script with others. Roleplaying is n excellent way to be certain that calls have the correct feel and help provide volunteers with confidence in relaying information about the candidate for whom they're working. This will also assure that callers can as they must be able to answer general questions without losing credibility.

Finally, closing phone calls properly can be not only be a way ensure a memorable and favorable impression, but may be required in some states to include a specific legal message. Be certain that such closing statements are carefully crafted and scripted according to the state requirements. Callers "going off script" are the easiest ways for a call to end in failure. In addition to meeting legal requirements, calls should end by mentioning once again the candidates name and the office they are seeking as well as

encouraging voters to support the candidate.

Precinct Walking

One of the campaigns most common uses for volunteers is the precinct walk. This is an opportunity to reach out to voters and connect with them face-to-face, and in this political campaign, these efforts are the heart of your campaign. Since a person's home is probably where they are the most comfortable (it is their turf), this is where they will share their ideas, their opinions and honest answers about whom they support in your race. Good Research and Organization are the keys to successful walks.

Research is again the key to this campaign strategy. Campaign staff should research vita precincts in the area or district using data from the local elections office in each jurisdiction.

➤ Keep a sign in sheet complete with volunteer addresses for thank you notes or cards.

➤ Good precincts are those that have high voter registration and good voter turnout in similar elections (Primaries, Generals).

➤ Precincts where similar candidates (Same party, etc...) have done well in past elections. Target Voters in selected precincts: (Using data from the Supervisor of Elections or "Victory Suite" © software from the Rep. Party, or other available software suite)

➤ Selected voters in a given precinct should be targeted (Voters who participate in similar elections: i.e. primary voters, presidential primary voters, etc...)

➤ Only plan to walk houses that have voters in the target group.

➤ Remember to have maps of areas that will be walked.

The campaign should also set a date or dates for precinct walks on days or at times that residents are at home such as evenings or on weekends.

Set a central meeting place near targeted precincts such as at a park or easy to find intersection. The campaign should have a member of the campaign staff at this location early to greet volunteers as they arrive and organize volunteers to walk. Volunteers who live in targeted precincts may better do evening walks, while weekend walks are more organized and require more volunteers to walk "specified areas."

Call on volunteers from the campaigns master volunteer list or contact organizations that support the campaign and have them send members or supporters. It is necessary to keep a list of those who commit to walk on specific dates and at specific times. A staff member will also need to follow-up with volunteers who commit to walk on select dates, as the date approaches (just to confirm their attendance).

Once at the location of n organized walk, meet volunteers and other walkers and have prepared walk lists with specific targeted addresses and resident names as well as a "walk script: that includes:

✓ Greeting

✓ Key points (issues) to mention

✓ Important Dates to disclose: Election Day

✓ Important Question: Can we count on your support? Record answers.

Walkers may also be given palm (push) cards with candidate information including phone numbers and as accurate mailing address.

Clip Boards, Pens, Yard signs and bumper stickers are good tools for each walker or walk-team to have as they approach potential supporters and voters.

To ensure that the campaign gets the most out of a walk, divide Volunteers into walk teams, ideally 2 persons each with one side of the street.

Each team should have an "odds" list by street name and an "evens" list by street name.

In cases where houses are too far apart to walk, three-person teams may be more effective.

✓ Odd list

✓ Even list

✓ Driver

At least one person should stay located at the central meeting place to assist "lost walkers" or walkers who arrive late, or finish an area earlier than expected. It may also help to interest walkers if there is some "incentive" at the central location. Such incentives may include refreshments, food or snacks.

Campaign volunteers or staffers should record the results of the walk. As volunteers return with walk sheets and recorded answers and notes about the target voters record the responses. It is beneficial to keep a record of how many supporters are in a given area, and who they are.

✓   How many supporters?

✓   How many opposed?

✓   How many undecided?

The responses can be used to generate GOTV (Get out the Vote) calls, or later follow-up calls to persuade undecided voters to support the candidate. Walkers may also note if supporters ask for yard signs or additional literature or if supporters in the area would like to volunteer to help out with other campaign activities.

When filing returned precinct information, data can best be file by precinct and all information on a given precinct should be kept together.

Precinct Walk Checklist

1. Research: Key Precincts in District _____

a. Use past election results

2. Research: Target Voters _____

a. Use Voter Lists

3. Print Walk Lists and Maps _____

4. Separate Walk Lists

    a. Walk-able areas in Targeted Precincts _____

    b. Even Side of Road _____

    c. Odd Side of Road _____

5. Create Walk Script

a. Greeting _____

b. Candidate info. _____

c. Tracking Question _____

6. Have Palm Cards/Hand-outs/Yard signs _____

7. Set Walk Date/Dates and times _____

8. Organize Volunteers:

a. Call Walkers from Volunteer list _____

b. Call Organizations to get volunteers _____

c. Keep a list of those who commit to walk _____

d. Follow-up with walkers to confirm _____

9. Set central meeting place _____

10. Set walk teams from volunteers "on-hand"

a. 2 or 3 person teams with lists _____

11. Walk:

a. Note responses to walkers _____

b. record walk data _____

c. establish walk follow-up plan

phone calls _____

ii. mailers _____

iii. GOTV plan _____

G.W. Pomichter

Election Day

In a well-run campaign, the final days and Election Day are the most anxious. This is in part because of the feeling of waiting, and in part because the campaign should have done almost all that is needed, and must wait to learn if voters have responded. There are, however, some final items to consider as the hours close in on the election results.

The campaign may consider using volunteers to make phone calls to identiofied supporters, or might pay a professional phone bank to call these supporters in a Get Out The Vote (GOTV) effort.

These supporting voters can be identified by frequent voters lists used throughout the campaign and should include all petition signers, all supporters identified through precinct walks, campaign events and other events.

Election Day Precinct Presence

Campaign volunteers should be stationed with signs at the entrance to key precincts on the day of the election. This could be the campaign's last opportunity to influence voters as they enter the polling place. The precincts that should be targeted will be established by using past elections data, and should include the top 20n precincts by turnout, or in a primary election the campaign may elect to staff the top 20 precincts by party registration and turn out. If the top 20 cannot be staffed adequately, the campaign should make every effort to have volunteers at as many as possible. There should be signs designated for each precinct to be placed on the night before the election. These signs will be placed on roads going into each polling place.

Public Events

Public appearances are vital to the survival of a political candidate. They may also be, due to the nature of candidates, an important part of keeping a candidate motivated through the arduous campaign process. Throughout the course of any campaign however it is critical to choose which events to attend. More crucial even, is deciding which events the candidate must or should attend, and which can be attended best by her spouse and which can be attended by a staff representative. Below are some helpful tips for choosing events for your campaign.

1. Events Attended by candidate:

a. Will candidate be allowed to speak to gathering, or is it more social? (Speaking opportunities are best)

b. Will any other candidates be present? (If yes, candidate may be best to attend to make counter-points to opposition)

c. Will Media be present? (If yes candidate should speak for him/her self)

d. How large is the group of event? (It is more valuable that The candidate attend larger events personally, to maximize exposure, let staff attend smaller events, as The candidate s time is better spent at larger events or on the phone raising funds {see Fund Raising}

e. Events attended by spouse:

f. Events that are gender specific and best attended by a spouse of the same gender as other attendees.

g. Events that are smaller, but more intimate in nature: tea-parties, Local family and community events

h. Events where a more intimate "(look)" at the candidate are expected.

2. Staff Events: (Staff should always accompany candidate when available and able, but should only attend specified events alone)

    a. Events where candidates are unable to speak but are expected to have a presence.

    b. Events held by smaller niche audiences, such as Home Owners associations, where a presence is helpful but not expected.

    c. Regularly scheduled events or meetings. (If possible the candidate might make a single appearance, but staff should be regularly in attendance when invited.)

The candidate's schedule is a limited and valuable resource, and should be guarded to insure that time is spent wisely. One simple rule to follow is to maximize the candidate's exposure while minimizing stress and opportunity for opposing candidates to attack your candidate's views.

Some candidates thrive on confrontation, but despite the allure of such public "battles" they are often counter-productive, unless they are properly planned for, and enjoy proper exposure to voters.

Check list for candidate Event -OR- speech

Location of Event: _____

Sponsor of Event: _____

Contact: _____

Address: _____

Directions: _____

MAP Attached: _____ YES _____ NO

Campaign Staff: _____

Attendance/Event Confirmed within the past 24 hours: _____

SPEECH DETAILS:

Topic of Speech: _____

Other Speakers: _____

_____

_____

Audience Size: _____

Audience is: CLUB ORGANIZATION OTHER: _____

Attendance List Available: _____

Materials on Hand:

Palm cards _____

Yard signs _____

Notebook _____

Other: _____

G.W. Pomichter

News Media

The relationship between political candidates and public officials and professional news journalists has always been a delicate balance of need and contempt. Often Media outlets have reputations for their political slants on issues. This perception of a biased media is often the cause for candidates and campaigns to avoid the media to their own detriment.

One of the first things the campaign will need is an up-to-date list of local and regional media outlets, as well as a general knowledge of the area "media market." These lists can be gathered by campaign volunteers or purchase through professional public relations services or campaign planners.

There are some important tips that make dealing with the media less agonizing and can help candidates and staffers to get the most out of the relationships they are able to build in the news community. These begin with understanding who and what members of the media are and include knowing the distinction between the message that a campaign is spreading and the purpose of the mass media, which is to provide information.

The most important thing to remember when working with news agencies is that they are populated with real people, and these people have opinions. While most journalists try to write accurate news stories, they do allow their own observations and sometimes opinions to influence their writing, so tread lightly. Often, journalists enter an interview or read a press release with an expectation they are being led. It is incumbent on each campaign to overcome such expectation by being as honest and open as possible, while remaining on message.

Another important factor in good media relations is a basic understanding that while political issues and public policy are the most important things to a candidate, a reporter must report the news that is important to his or her readers. Candidates should be aware of how their points of view affect newspaper readers and news agency customers. It is important to know the audience that the campaign is trying to reach, and to focus on delivering the campaign message in a way that is of greatest interest.

While there are some hostile organizations or individual reporters, most are doing the job that they were hired to do and for which they have a passion not unlike the candidate's passion for service. They are news reporters, not public relations specialist. The most effective way to communicate with them is completely, honestly and with an eye toward the information that the candidate wants reported.

In most cases, news articles are not "spun" at the news bureau or by individual reporters, they are "pre-spun" by the subjects.

It is also important to remember that we live in a sound bite society, not for any other reason, but that most readers, TV watchers and radio listeners are people with busy lives and have little time to dedicate to your message. News mediums are also space limited, and must fit complex ideas into small packages, so while public policy issues are complicated, the positions of a candidate must be compacted for consumption. (It is helpful to pre-boil positions down to series of "bite-sized" comments that accurately, but briefly describe positions.)

To build effective and continuing relationships with the news community compile and keep an accurate list of all community, local, state and when applicable national media outlets, and the name of a good contact person (reporter). Professional Media relations persons spend years learning to communicate effectively with reporters, and building lasting contacts so on larger more involved campaigns it is often a good idea to have a professional media consultant.

Once you understand these simple if often hard to accept facts, there are some rules of engagement that you and your candidate should follow.

Media Tips

The media is an important campaign tool, particularly when resources are scarce. Earned media, or "press" coverage is a great way to share the campaign message with area voters.

Some basic rules apply to using the earned media to disseminate campaign information.

The candidate should be the primary spokes-person for the campaign; as it is the candidate that needs the exposure, and that can best articulate the official opinions of the campaign. Volunteers and staff members should avoid any spontaneous interactions with the earned media community, and if staffers are asked in advance to make statements, they should have prepared "statements" that ALL staff uses consistently. It is important to remember that while staff may have similar opinions to a candidate, they may not have identical opinions or may not articulate these opinions as concisely as the candidate.

1. Be polite and always gracious and keep composure. Some personalities simply do not "click," but when an argumentative reporter can affect the candidate,

they will. Being off balance clouds a candidates mind, and can force confused or irrational answers, and can lead to grammatical errors that make embarrassing sound bites.

2. Nothing is off the record. It is the job of a reporter to report ANY interesting, unusual or news worthy item, so do not say anything that you don't want printed, aired or otherwise exposed. A common misconception about news media is that anything that a candidate deems as "off-the-record," won't be printed or broadcast. This isn't true. If an opinion is not fully developed or requires "off-the-record" thought or discussion, these should take place well in advance of any media contact. Only thoroughly thought out points should be discussed in the presence of members of the media.

3. Always speak in brief statements and as grammatically correct as possible. Do not be rushed or pressured by reporters, give thought to your answers or comments, and speak clearly and

correctly. (Nothing sounds worse than an otherwise educated candidate who confuses verb tense, or speaks in fragmented sentences, particularly on camera or tape where there may be NO editor to help out.)

If your interview is recorded by video or audiotape, try to have some prior notice, and give some thought to the issues you may be asked to respond to.

Make sure that the candidate does not speak over the heads of reporters or their readers or customers. (This can cause clarity to be lost, and voters to become confused, often mistaking the candidate's position on issues.)

Keep reporters on target and on message. Like lawyers, reporters often ask the same question in many different ways to solicit different responses or gauge the candidate's consistency. They may also try to steer the interview, recognize this and maintain your message.

When writing press releases it is handy to know what news agencies are looking for.

1.	JUST the Who, What, When and Where: ONE SHORT page.

2.	Give contact phone number for follow-up

3.	Give some background, not an excessive amount, reporters that want more will call, but in the event that the release is deemed as just a "brief," then a "just the basics" release will make news staff's job easier and will be appreciated.

Candidate Media Interview

Interviewing Organization: _____

Name of Interviewer: _____

Interview Topic: _____

Interview Location/Address: _____

Detailed MAP Attached: _____
On Hand:
Press Packet: _____
Printed Materials _____
Candidate Photo _____
Campaign contact Info. _____
Candidate Readiness:
Hand Mirror _____
Comb/Brush _____
Proper Attire/Prepared for photo _____
Lint Brush _____

Candidate TV/Radio interview
Station: _____
Radio Host: _____
TV/Radio Demographic Info:_____
LOCATION/MAP: _____

Candidate T.V. Interview
Candidate (Blue Shirt, Non-busy Tie, Primary Colors): _____
Materials memorized No printed materials during interview _____
Answers/Statements short: 15-20 seconds _____

STAY ON MESSAGE!

G.W. Pomichter

Campaign Ethics

It has been said, "a person's character is their destiny." If this profound statement is true, then it is perhaps very important that as we discuss campaigns we take a few moments to discuss the ethics of campaigning. For many, the candidate's personal ethics and convictions are the heart of their reason for running for public office and must be weighed and measured as an overall part of the campaign strategy.

The Constitution of The United States and fifty state constitutions outline a plan for the peaceful transfer of power through elections. This process, however peaceful, is a struggle for the ability of individuals to serve the masses, and can best be understood as a battle for power. For this reason, the ethics and terms of the conflict should be those commonly used in such a battle. Like any civilized conflict though, there are some ethical obligations to campaign warfare. Contrary to so much popular opinion, public service is an honorable goal, and a dignified profession and candidates and staffers on both sides of the battlefield should conduct themselves appropriately.

It is important as we take the field of battle that we acknowledge some painful and stubborn facts. The first is that while tempers often flare in the heat of debate and discourses, with rare exception, most of those who choose to enter public service and to campaign to hold an office of public trust, do so with the very best intentions. Politicians are quite often dreamers and idealists who have a genuine desire to serve the best interests of the people, in a manner that they perceive as best, even our opponents. Once we understand this, we can more appropriately act during our campaign.

There is a natural tendency within the campaign to vilify our adversaries. This is to be expected and is an appropriate tactic for building our team's espri-dé-corps. This vilification, however, should be limited to the campaign's parameters, and not taken so seriously as to transform an honorable contest into a more barbaric street scene. Politics can fire tempers, especially for those loyalists in each candidate's "camp", and while most end in the graceful defeat of opposition, it is not unheard of for political idealism to lead to open riot if cooler more controlled behaviors do not prevail.

It is important to recall that the U.S. political process is an experiment in democratic and peaceful elections. It was born in a time when struggles for political supremacy were fought with bullets and bayonets and very often yielded bloody and unpopular results.

Today, the peaceful transition of power from one leader to the next, and sometimes from one ideology to the next is a testament to the success of America's electoral process. This success relies heavily on the ethical conduct of participants in any political contest. For this reason, it is incumbent on every candidate to draw boundaries and establish a code of conduct that will temper a spirited debate and discourse while preventing the kinds of overzealous extremism that have typically yielded hateful and sometimes even violent results in other nations of the world.

Negative Campaigning

The most basic battles are fought between candidates because of their ideas of leadership for their perspective constituencies, and a commonly used method of advertising, to compare each candidate and their individual vision for the office in question, is not unfair; in fact, this should be the primary combat tactic engaged in by both sides. This is not negative campaigning. It is commonly referred to as a comparison piece or advertisement.

A negative campaign ad or strategy, one that capitalizes on the personal flaws of one's opponent, is however a part of the American political landscape, and while many in the general population claim that these are pointless attacks on the character of otherwise honest candidates, the fact remains that they still work effectively.

If a candidate so vehemently refuses to engage in any negative campaigning, than often times they will suffer defeat—not because of any single issue or position, but as victims of the public perceptions that can too often sway elections.

Because the way each candidate is perceived will play a vital role in their victory or defeat, an ad or other medium that points out distinctions between candidates or highlights a particular persons flaws may be the only thing standing between your candidate and a missed opportunity to do the job they are asking the public to bestow on them. Regardless of their best intentions, a defeated candidate will not serve the public in office.

Some rules to think about:

✓   Be on message. Always consider the scope of a negative advertisement. Is it appropriate? Does it have bearing on the public's perception of the office?

✓   Be honorable. Always verify that statements about opponents are TRUE and be able to document the facts. Public service is an honorable profession and should be taken up by honorable people.

✓   Be professional. Limit statements to the subject at hand: your opponent and his views, not to outsiders who have not chosen to participate in the election or to close family and friends who are, in battle field words, non-combatants.

✓   Be cautious. No person is without flaw, and it is important that your candidate be prepared to answer about any issue or topic that is raised by your advertisement.

✓   Be gracious. A negative strategy or as some call them attack ads are a weapon of much destruction. They can lead to ill will between peaceful rivals, and can have other long lasting effects on opponents. For this reason they should be considered weapons of last resort, not to be used carelessly, or maliciously.

Once you have met this handful of litmus tests, and your campaign is prepared for battle, be victorious!

SAMPLE CAMPAIGN COUNTDOWN CALENDAR

SUNDAY	MONDAY	TUESDAY	WEDNESDAY	THURSDAY	FRIDAY	SATURDAY
< PLAN Fundraising already in progress **F** **undraising**	Campaign Leaders Meeting	**Fundraising**	**Fundraising**	**Fundraising**	**Fundraising**	Campaign Kickoff: Volunteer sign-up
Commercial and Yard Sign Placement Begins	**Fundraising**		**Fundraising**	**Fundraising**		**Fundraising**
Campaign Team Meeting **Fundraising**	Precinct Walk **Fundraising**	Precinct Walk **Fundraising**	Precinct Walk **Fundraising**	Precinct Walk **Fundraising**		Precinct Walk Sign Waive
P.M. Precinct Walk	Commercial Signs placed **Fundraising**	21-DAY COUNTDOWN **Fundraising** Evening Walk	Larger **Office** Radio/TV Saturation Begins **Fundraising**	*Morning* *Waive* **Fundraising** *Evening* *Walk*	*Morning* *Waive* **Fundraising** *Evening* *Walk*	Precinct Walk Sign Waive

Mapping the Road Less Traveled

P.M. Precinct Walk	1A Split Mailer Drop *Morning Waive* **Evening Walk**	1A Split Mailer arrives *Morning Waive* **Evening Walk**	*Morning Waive* **Evening Sign Waive** *Evening Walk*	AB Mailer Drop *Morning Waive* **Evening Walk**	AB Mailer arrives *Morning Waive* **Evening Walk**	recinct Walk Sign Waive
Precinct Walk	**Smaller Office** Radio/TV Saturation Begins where applicable	2AB Mailer Drop *Morning Waive*	2AB Mailer Arrives 2A Split Mailer Drop **Evening Sign Waive**	2 A Split Mailer Arr. *Morning Waive*	Last Mailer Drop	Largest Sign Waive Precinct Walk
	Large Sign Waive Precinct Walk		Last Mailer arrives *A.M. Waive* Yard-signs at all precincts by 2 a.m.		**Election Day** Sign Waive at top 10 Precincts	

137

G.W. Pomichter

The information contained in this book has been compiled to assist both professional and first-time candidates, campaign manager an campaign staff members. It is not intended to replace a professional campaign manager or consultant, and candidates should use their best judgment in implementing these strategies. I sincerely recommend engaging a professional campaign manager to best implement the strategies contained herein.

**G.W. Pomichter